FINDING MOTIVATION IN DESPONDENCY

COPING WITH DIFFICULT TIMES

DR. JAGADEESH PILLAI

|| Dedicated to all wisdom seekers around the World ||

♡♡♡

Contents

Contents

Prayer

"Om Bhadram Karnebhih Shrunuyaama
DevaahBhadram Pashyemaakshabhiryajatraah
SthirairangaistushtuvaamsastanoobhihVyashema
Devahitam YadaayuhSwasti Na Indro
VridhashravaahSwasti Nah Pooshaa
VishwavedaahSwasti Nastaarkshyo ArishtanemihSwasti
No Brihaspatir DadhaatuOm Shantih, Shantih, Shantih"

The literal meaning of this mantra is: OM. O Gods! Let us hear auspicious words from our ears. O reverent Gods! Let us behold propitious visions from our eyes, let our organs and body be stable, healthy, and strong. Let us do that which is pleasing to the gods in the life span allotted to us. May Indra, inscribed in the scriptures, bring us fortune! May Pushan, the knower of the world, grant us prosperity! May Trakshya, who vanquishes enemies, bestow us with blessings! May Brihaspati bring us success!
OM Peace, Peace, Peace.

༄༄༄

About The Author

Dr. Jagadeesh Pillai is a renowned Guinness World Record holder, writer, and researcher hailing from Varanasi, also known as the abode of Lord Shiva. With a Ph.D. in Vedic Science and a range of creative ideas and achievements, he is a true polymath. He is the author of more than 100 books including Research Publications. Although his roots can be traced back to Kerala, the people of Varanasi hold him in high regard and affectionately consider him one of their own.

In 1998, Dr. Pillai was offered a job at Banaras Hindu University, but he left the position after only two months to pursue greater goals in life. He believed that in order to study Indian scriptures and engage in other creative endeavours, he needed to retire from the daily grind of working solely for money at a young age.

He started an export business from scratch, using the knowledge he had gained from a previous job in the industry. His intelligence and unique approach to business led to great success in a short period of time, earning him more in just a decade and a half than he would have in a lifetime working in a government job. Upon the passing of Dr. APJ Abdul Kalam, Dr. Pillai decided to leave the business and dedicate himself to reading, studying, researching, and experimenting.

During his tenure in the export business, Dr. Pillai traveled to over 16 countries, gaining valuable insight and experiencing the world and life in detail.

Dr. Pillai has achieved four Guinness World Records in the following subjects:

"Script to Screen" - In this record, Dr. Pillai produced and directed an animation film within the shortest time possible, breaking the previous record set by Canadians. He has also received numerous national and international awards and recognitions for this achievement.

Longest Line of Postcards - For this record, Dr. Pillai created a line of 16,300 postcards on the occasion of the 163rd anniversary of Indian Postal Day. The event also included a questionnaire about the Indian flag.

Largest Poster Awareness Campaign - Dr. Pillai designed an awareness campaign on the subject of "Beti Bachao - Beti Padhao" (Save the Girl Child - Educate the Girl Child) to achieve this record.

Largest Envelope - In tribute to the Indian Prime Minister's "Make in India" initiative, Dr. Pillai created a 4000 square meter envelope using waste paper to achieve this record.

Attempted - **70000 Candles on a 210 kg Cake** - To celebrate the 70th Indian Independence Day, Dr. Pillai attempted to light 70,000 candles on a 210 kg cake, which was recorded in World Records India.

Attempted - **Documentary on Dhamek Stupa of Sarnath in 17 Languages** - Dr. Pillai attempted to create a documentary on the Dhamek Stupa of Sarnath, dubbing it in 17 different languages. The result of this attempt is currently awaiting confirmation from the Guinness World Records.

Dr. Pillai is skilled in teaching the Bhagavad Gita, a Hindu scripture, and is popular among young people. He has helped many young people improve their lives through his motivational teachings.

In addition to teaching, he has composed and sung numerous Sanskrit Bhajans and patriotic songs.

He has also written and directed several short films and documentaries for awareness campaigns, and has volunteered with the police in both UP and Kerala to spread awareness about various issues through videos and photography.

Incredibly, he has produced and directed over 100 documentaries about the city of Varanasi, all on his own.

He has also helped and guided more than 25 boys and girls to achieve world records through creative and innovative methods. He is a multifaceted person who uses his intellect and the blessings given to him by God to excel in various areas. He is both a teacher and a student, always learning and teaching, and is able to master any subject he comes across.

He is a selfless social activist and motivational speaker who has overcome struggles and failures to become a successful and enthusiastic individual with a rich life experience.

In addition to his work with the Bhagavad Gita, he is also an efficient Tarot card reader, Astro-Vastu consultant, and a talented singer and composer. He has sung the entire Ram Charita Manas and Bhagavad Gita in his own compositions, and has sung the phrase "Lokah Samastha Sukhino Bhavantu" in 50 different languages. He is currently working on a detailed and scientific study of Vedas, Upanishads, Puranas, and the Bhagavad Gita. He has also composed and sung the Hanuman Chalisa and Gayatri Mantra in 108 and 1008 different compositions, respectively.

Awards - Four Times Guinness World Records, Winner of Mahatma Gandhi Vishwa Shanti Puraskar, Mahatma Gandhi Global Peace Ambassador, Kashi Ratna Award, Dr. APJ Abdul Kalam Motivational Person of the Year 2017, Mother Teresa Award, Indira Gandhi Priyadarshini Award, Bharat Vikas Ratna Award, Udyog Ratna Award, Vigyan Prasar Award, Poorvanchal Ratn Samman.

ᗉᗉᗉ

Preface

The journey of life is not always smooth and often we face difficult times that can leave us feeling defeated, overwhelmed, and despondent. Whether it's the loss of a loved one, a major life transition, or a personal setback, it can be challenging to find the motivation and strength to keep moving forward.

However, it is during these challenging times that our resilience and inner strength is tested, and it is important to understand that we have the power to change our outlook and find the motivation to persevere. This is where the book "Finding Motivation in Despondency: Coping with Difficult Times" comes in.

This book is a comprehensive guide to understanding and overcoming negative emotions and feelings of despondency. It provides practical tools and strategies for managing stress, anxiety, and other negative emotions, and for building resilience and inner strength. With a focus on positive thinking, gratitude, and self-care, this book provides the motivation and support needed to persevere through difficult times.

Through this book, you will learn the power of setting realistic goals, connecting with others, and finding meaning and purpose in life. You will gain insight into the role of mindfulness and self-compassion in managing negative emotions, and you will develop the tools needed to overcome procrastination, perfectionism, and other challenges that can keep you stuck.

With its actionable advice and inspiration, "Finding Motivation in Despondency: Coping with Difficult Times" is an essential resource for anyone facing difficult times and seeking to find the motivation and resilience to keep moving forward. Whether you are navigating a personal crisis, dealing with the loss of a loved one, or simply looking for ways to cope with the ups and downs of life, this book will provide the guidance and support you need.

So, if you are ready to embrace change and find motivation in despondency, then this book is for you. Whether you are reading it on your own or with a friend, this guide will help you to develop the inner strength, resilience, and motivation you need to persevere through difficult times.

ᕈᕈᕈ

ONE

Introduction Understanding Motivation and its Importance in Difficult Times

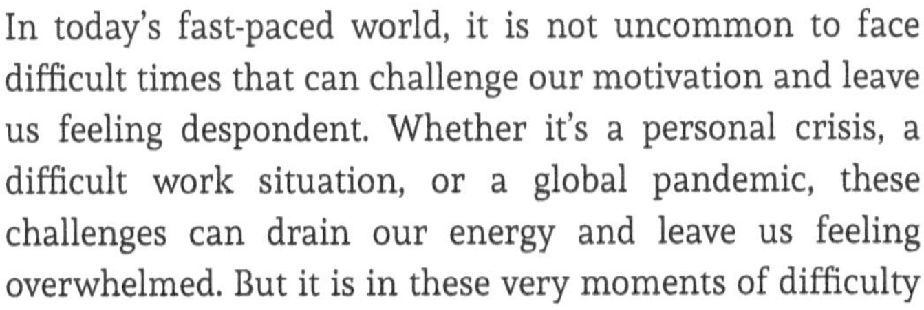

In today's fast-paced world, it is not uncommon to face difficult times that can challenge our motivation and leave us feeling despondent. Whether it's a personal crisis, a difficult work situation, or a global pandemic, these challenges can drain our energy and leave us feeling overwhelmed. But it is in these very moments of difficulty that motivation becomes even more important.

Motivation is a critical component of resilience and helps

us overcome obstacles and achieve our goals. Without motivation, it can be challenging to stay focused, motivated, and productive during tough times. In this chapter, we will examine what motivation is, how it works, and why it is crucial in difficult times.

We will explore different theories of motivation, including self-determination theory and intrinsic and extrinsic motivation, and discuss how these theories can help us better understand why we are motivated or demotivated in certain situations. We will also discuss the relationship between motivation and emotions, and how our emotions can impact our level of motivation.

Finally, we will look at the importance of motivation in difficult times, and how it can help us to remain optimistic and focused, even in the face of adversity. We will also discuss the role that self-care, self-compassion, and positive self-talk can play in fostering motivation and resilience in difficult times.

By the end of this chapter, readers will have a better understanding of what motivation is, how it works, and why it is critical in difficult times. They will also have an appreciation for the importance of self-care, self-compassion, and positive self-talk in maintaining motivation and resilience during tough times.

ppp

"The greatest glory in living lies not in never falling, but in rising every time we fall."

-Nelson Mandela

ᗡᗡᗡ

TWO

RECOGNIZING AND MANAGING NEGATIVE EMOTIONS

Negative emotions such as anger, fear, sadness, and frustration are a normal part of life. They can be triggered by a wide range of events, including financial stress, relationship problems, health issues, and other life challenges. While it is impossible to completely eliminate negative emotions, it is possible to learn how to manage them effectively.

One of the first steps in managing negative emotions is to recognize them when they arise. This can involve paying attention to physical sensations in the body, such as tightness in the chest or knots in the stomach, as well as changes in mood, such as irritability or restlessness.

Once you have recognized a negative emotion, it is important to take a step back and assess the situation. Ask yourself questions such as "What am I feeling?", "What triggered this emotion?", and "How can I respond in a healthy way?". By taking this time to reflect, you can gain a better understanding of the situation and find ways to cope with the negative emotion.

One effective strategy for managing negative emotions is to engage in relaxation techniques, such as deep breathing, meditation, or yoga. These activities can help to calm the body and reduce physical symptoms associated with stress and anxiety.

In addition, it is important to find healthy outlets for expressing negative emotions, such as talking to a trusted friend or loved one, journaling, or participating in a creative activity like painting or drawing. Avoiding activities that may perpetuate negative feelings, such as substance abuse or engaging in negative self-talk.

It is also essential to practice self-care, such as getting regular exercise, eating a nutritious diet, and getting adequate sleep. By taking care of yourself, you can help to build resilience and reduce the impact of negative emotions.

Finally, it is important to remember that negative emotions are a natural and necessary part of life, and it is okay to feel them. By embracing and managing negative emotions in a healthy way, we can learn from them, grow, and find motivation in even the most difficult of times.

ppp

"Hardships often prepare ordinary people for
an extraordinary destiny."

-C.S. Lewis

ᗡᗡᗡ

THREE

SETTING REALISTIC GOALS AND PRIORITIZING SELF-CARE

In order to maintain our mental and emotional wellbeing, it is important to set realistic goals for ourselves and prioritize self-care. Goals that are too unrealistic can set us up for failure and trigger feelings of disappointment, frustration, and inadequacy. On the other hand, setting achievable goals and tracking our progress can give us a sense of accomplishment and boost our motivation and self-esteem.

Self-care is another key aspect of managing negative emotions and maintaining mental and emotional wellbeing. Self-care can include activities such as exercise, meditation, and spending time with friends and family. Engaging in self-care helps us to reduce stress and anxiety, process and manage difficult emotions in a healthy way, and foster a sense of self-love and self-acceptance.

Additionally, it is important to set aside time for self-reflection and introspection. By reflecting on our experiences, we can gain a deeper understanding of our emotions and thoughts, and gain a clearer perspective on our lives. This can help us to manage negative emotions and feel more in control of our lives.

Setting realistic goals and prioritizing self-care can help us to maintain our motivation and stay focused on our objectives, even in difficult times. By taking care of ourselves and setting achievable goals, we can maintain our mental and emotional wellbeing and find the motivation to keep moving forward.

It is also important to celebrate small victories and acknowledge our accomplishments along the way. This can help to build confidence and a sense of achievement, and provide motivation to continue pursuing our goals. Additionally, seeking support from friends, family, or a therapist can provide a sounding board and encouragement as we work towards our objectives. Remember, it is okay to seek help and it is a sign of strength to admit when we need support. By setting realistic goals, prioritizing self-care, and seeking support, we can cultivate the resilience and inner strength needed to navigate difficult times and achieve our aspirations.

ϷϷϷ

"Success is not final, failure is not fatal: it is the courage to continue that counts."

-Winston Churchill

ᗡᗡᗡ

FOUR

Building Resilience and Coping with Setbacks

Building resilience and coping with setbacks are critical skills for navigating difficult times. Resilience refers to the ability to bounce back from adverse experiences and to continue moving forward despite challenges. This ability can be developed and strengthened with practice, and is key to maintaining a positive outlook and finding motivation in difficult times.

Setting realistic goals and prioritizing self-care are essential for building resilience. When faced with setbacks, it can be tempting to give up or to become discouraged. However, by setting achievable goals and focusing on self-care, you can cultivate the strength and perseverance necessary to overcome obstacles and achieve success.

In order to build resilience, it is important to recognize and manage negative emotions. Negative emotions such as anxiety, fear, and anger can be overwhelming and can interfere with our ability to think clearly and make sound decisions. However, by learning to identify and manage these emotions in a healthy way, we can build the emotional resilience necessary to face challenges with confidence and optimism.

Additionally, it is important to practice self-compassion. Self-compassion involves treating ourselves with the same kindness, understanding, and care that we would offer to a dear friend. This can help to foster a more positive self-image and to reduce feelings of stress and anxiety during difficult times.

Moreover, it is important to be proactive in seeking support when necessary. Having a supportive network of friends and family can provide comfort and encouragement during difficult times. Additionally, therapy and other forms of mental health support can be valuable resources for building resilience and coping with setbacks.

Finally, it is important to focus on the present moment and to take things one day at a time. While it can be tempting to dwell on the past or to worry about the future, it is important to stay focused on the present and to find joy in the little things in life. This can help to reduce stress and anxiety and to cultivate the resilience and positive outlook necessary to navigate difficult times with grace and optimism.

In conclusion, building resilience and coping with setbacks are critical skills for finding motivation and overcoming difficult times. By focusing on self-care, setting realistic goals, and seeking support when necessary, we can develop the emotional resilience necessary to face challenges with confidence and optimism.

"Never give up on a dream just because of the time it will take to accomplish it. The time will pass anyway."

-Earl Nightingale

FIVE

OVERCOMING PROCRASTINATION AND PERFECTIONISM

One of the major obstacles to motivation and success is procrastination and perfectionism. These tendencies can hold us back and prevent us from reaching our full potential. To overcome them, it's important to understand the root causes and develop effective strategies.

Procrastination is often rooted in fear of failure, fear of success, or simply a lack of motivation. Perfectionism can stem from a fear of not measuring up or a need to control outcomes. Both of these tendencies can lead to a cycle of self-doubt, frustration, and inactivity.

To overcome procrastination and perfectionism, it's important to adopt a growth mindset and focus on progress rather than perfection. Set realistic, achievable goals and break them down into manageable tasks. Prioritize self-care and self-compassion to reduce stress and anxiety and increase resilience.

It can also be helpful to challenge negative self-talk and practice positive self-affirmations. Finally, consider seeking support from friends, family, or a mental health professional to help you navigate these obstacles.

In conclusion, procrastination and perfectionism are common barriers to motivation and success, but with the right tools and strategies, they can be overcome. By focusing on progress, prioritizing self-care, and seeking support, you can break free from these tendencies and move towards a more fulfilling and motivated life.

ϸϸϸ

"In every difficult situation is potential value."

-Eckhart Tolle

♥♥♥

SIX

Understanding the Power of Positive Thinking and Gratitude

The power of positive thinking and gratitude cannot be overstated, especially during difficult times. Negative thoughts and feelings can easily take hold, making it difficult to find motivation and cope with challenges. On the other hand, a positive mindset and an attitude of gratitude can help to boost our mood, increase our resilience, and improve our overall wellbeing.

Positive thinking involves focusing on the good things in life and actively looking for the positive in difficult situations. It requires shifting our focus away from negative thoughts and feelings and toward positive thoughts and emotions. This can be a difficult habit to develop, but with practice, it becomes easier.

Gratitude, or the practice of being thankful for what we have, can also have a profound impact on our mental and emotional wellbeing. Taking time each day to reflect on the things we are grateful for can help to put things into perspective and to appreciate what we have in our lives. This shift in perspective can help to counteract negative emotions and foster a more positive outlook on life.

It is important to remember that positive thinking and gratitude are not about ignoring or denying difficult situations and emotions. Rather, they are about acknowledging these challenges and working to find the good in them. By doing so, we can build resilience and increase our ability to cope with difficult times.

In conclusion, the power of positive thinking and gratitude is significant and should not be underestimated. By developing a positive mindset and an attitude of gratitude, we can improve our wellbeing and find the motivation to overcome even the most difficult challenges.

ᎠᎠᎠ

"You may encounter many defeats, but you must not be defeated. In fact, it may be necessary to encounter the defeats, so you can know who you are, what you can rise from, how you can still come out of it."

-Maya Angelou

♡♡♡

SEVEN

BUILDING SUPPORT SYSTEMS AND CONNECTING WITH OTHERS

The importance of building support systems and connecting with others cannot be overstated when it comes to coping with difficult times. Having a strong support system can provide a source of comfort and encouragement during challenging moments, and can also help you to develop a more positive outlook on life. In addition, connecting with others can help you to feel less isolated, and to gain new perspectives on the difficulties you are facing.

One way to build a support system is by reaching out to

family and friends. You may also want to consider joining a support group, or seeking out therapy or counseling. It can also be helpful to engage in activities that allow you to connect with others who share similar interests or challenges, such as volunteering, participating in a club, or attending events.

It is also important to prioritize self-care and to make time for activities that bring you joy and help you to unwind. This can include exercise, meditation, reading, or spending time in nature. By taking care of yourself, you can increase your resilience and better cope with the challenges that life presents.

In conclusion, building support systems and connecting with others can play a critical role in coping with difficult times. By reaching out for help, prioritizing self-care, and participating in activities that bring you joy, you can increase your resilience and find the motivation you need to overcome even the most difficult of challenges.

ᗊᗊᗊ

"Hope is not a strategy. It's a source of power,
of energy, of vitality."

-Robert H. Schuller

♡♡♡

EIGHT

FINDING PURPOSE AND MEANING IN DIFFICULT TIMES

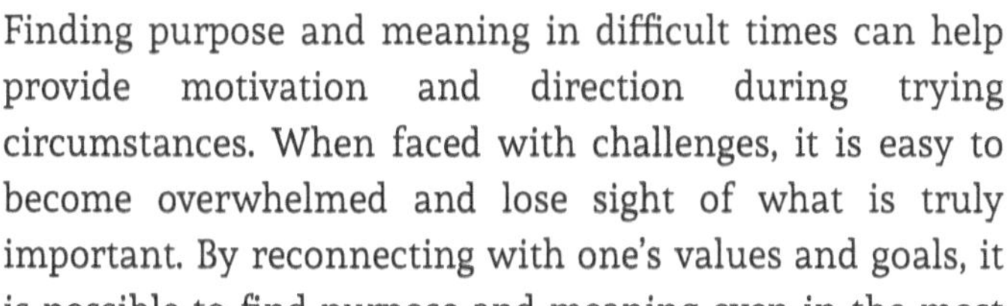

Finding purpose and meaning in difficult times can help provide motivation and direction during trying circumstances. When faced with challenges, it is easy to become overwhelmed and lose sight of what is truly important. By reconnecting with one's values and goals, it is possible to find purpose and meaning even in the most difficult times.

One way to do this is by setting realistic and meaningful goals, such as volunteering, pursuing a new hobby, or working on personal growth. Another approach is to engage in activities that bring joy and fulfillment, such as spending time with loved ones, taking care of oneself through self-care, or helping others in need.

It is also important to seek support from others, including friends, family, and professional support systems such as therapy. Talking through difficult emotions and experiences with others can help to provide a new perspective and bring a sense of hope and direction.

Additionally, practicing gratitude and focusing on what one has rather than what one lacks can also provide a sense of purpose and meaning. This can include keeping a gratitude journal, meditating on positive experiences, or expressing gratitude to others.

Ultimately, finding purpose and meaning in difficult times requires a commitment to self-reflection, personal growth, and a willingness to embrace change. By taking small steps and seeking support when needed, it is possible to not only cope with difficult times, but to also find meaning and motivation amidst the challenges.

ᗞᗞᗞ

"The only way to do great work is to love what you do."

-Steve Jobs

♡♡♡

NINE

MANAGING STRESS AND ANXIETY

Stress and anxiety can be overwhelming and detrimental to our emotional wellbeing. In times of difficulty, it is essential to prioritize self-care and find healthy ways to manage these emotions. Some strategies for managing stress and anxiety include:

Exercise: Regular physical activity can help to release tension and reduce stress levels.

Mindfulness and meditation: Engaging in mindfulness activities can help to calm the mind and reduce feelings of anxiety.

Time management: By organizing our time and setting realistic goals, we can reduce stress levels and feel more in control.

Talking to someone: Sharing our experiences and feelings with a trusted friend, family member, or mental health professional can help to process and manage stress and anxiety.

Taking breaks: Taking regular breaks from daily activities can help to recharge and reduce stress levels.

Seeking professional help: If stress and anxiety become overwhelming, it may be helpful to seek the support of a mental health professional.

By incorporating these strategies into our daily routine, we can reduce stress and anxiety levels, and foster a sense of emotional wellbeing.

ԹԹԹ

"The only way out of the labyrinth of
suffering is to forgive."

-John Green

♥♥♥

TEN

THE ROLE OF MINDFULNESS AND SELF-COMPASSION

Mindfulness and self-compassion are two essential tools that can help individuals in difficult times to manage their emotions and overcome feelings of stress, anxiety, and despondency. Mindfulness involves being present in the moment and focusing on one's thoughts and emotions, while self-compassion involves treating oneself with kindness and understanding, especially during difficult times.

Studies have shown that incorporating mindfulness practices into one's daily routine can help reduce stress and anxiety levels and improve overall emotional wellbeing. This can include simple practices such as deep breathing, meditation, and yoga. Self-compassion, on the other hand, can help individuals to view their struggles and setbacks in a more positive light, leading to greater resilience and the ability to cope with difficulties.

Additionally, practicing mindfulness and self-compassion can help to foster a sense of connection with oneself, leading to greater self-awareness and a deeper understanding of one's motivations and emotions. This can be particularly helpful in difficult times when individuals may feel disconnected from themselves or overwhelmed by negative emotions.

Incorporating mindfulness and self-compassion into one's daily routine can be a powerful tool in finding motivation and hope during difficult times. It is essential to remember that these practices take time and patience to develop, and it is important to be gentle with oneself as you begin to incorporate them into your life.

ppp

"When the going gets tough, the tough get going."

ᗡᗡᗡ

ELEVEN

DEALING WITH FAILURE AND LEARNING FROM MISTAKES

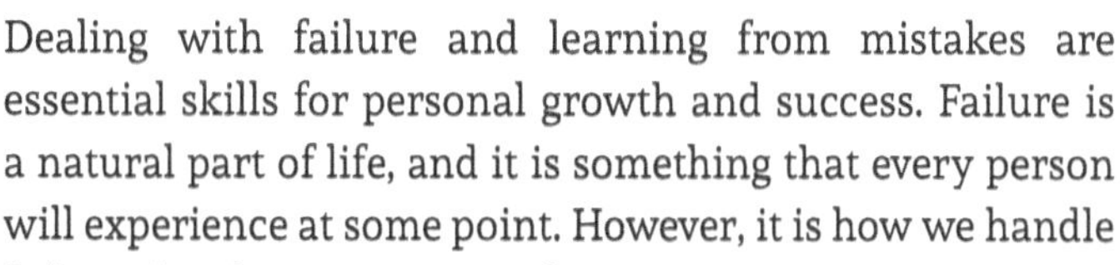

Dealing with failure and learning from mistakes are essential skills for personal growth and success. Failure is a natural part of life, and it is something that every person will experience at some point. However, it is how we handle failure that determines our ultimate success.

One of the first steps in dealing with failure is to accept it. Failure is not a reflection of our self-worth, but rather a learning opportunity. It is important to acknowledge that failure is a part of the process and not to beat ourselves up over it.

Next, it is important to analyze the situation and identify what went wrong. This can be done by asking ourselves questions such as: What were the contributing factors to the failure? What could I have done differently? What can I learn from this experience?

Once we have identified the root cause of the failure, we can take action to prevent it from happening again. This can involve making changes to our approach, seeking out advice from others, or gaining new knowledge or skills.

It is also important to remember that failure is not final. We can always try again and learn from our mistakes. In fact, it is often through failure that we learn the most and grow the most.

Lastly, it is essential to not dwell on failure and instead focus on moving forward. We should not let failure define us or limit our potential. We should use the lessons learned from failure to improve ourselves and our performance.

In conclusion, dealing with failure and learning from mistakes are crucial skills for personal growth and success. By accepting failure, analyzing the situation, taking action, and focusing on moving forward, we can turn failure into a valuable learning opportunity.

"We may encounter many defeats but we
must not be defeated."

-Maya Angelou

♡♡♡

TWELVE

UNDERSTANDING AND MANAGING TRAUMA

Trauma is a distressing event that can have a significant impact on a person's mental and emotional well-being. Trauma can result from various experiences, such as physical or sexual abuse, natural disasters, car accidents, or military combat. Understanding and managing trauma is crucial for recovery and healing.

The first step in managing trauma is to seek professional help, such as a therapist or counselor who specializes in trauma treatment. Therapy can provide a safe space to process and work through the trauma and its aftermath.

It is also important to take care of oneself. This can include engaging in self-care activities such as exercise, mindfulness, or hobbies. Developing a support system of friends and family who understand and support the journey towards recovery can also be helpful.

Another important aspect of managing trauma is to learn coping mechanisms and techniques to manage symptoms. This can include techniques such as deep breathing, progressive muscle relaxation, and visualization. Keeping a journal can also be a helpful tool in processing the trauma and tracking progress.

It is also crucial to address any negative thoughts and beliefs that may have developed as a result of the trauma. These thoughts can be changed through cognitive-behavioral therapy, which helps to reframe negative thinking patterns.

In addition, it is important to recognize and understand triggers. Triggers are experiences or events that bring back memories or emotions associated with the trauma. By becoming aware of triggers, individuals can work to manage their reactions and minimize the impact of the triggers.

In conclusion, managing trauma requires a comprehensive approach that includes seeking professional help, self-care, learning coping mechanisms, addressing negative thoughts, and managing triggers. With time and support, individuals can overcome trauma and reclaim their lives.

ﭫﭫﭫ

"The most important thing is to enjoy your
life - to be happy - it's all that matters."

-Audrey Hepburn

♡♡♡

THIRTEEN

BUILDING INNER STRENGTH THROUGH ADVERSITY

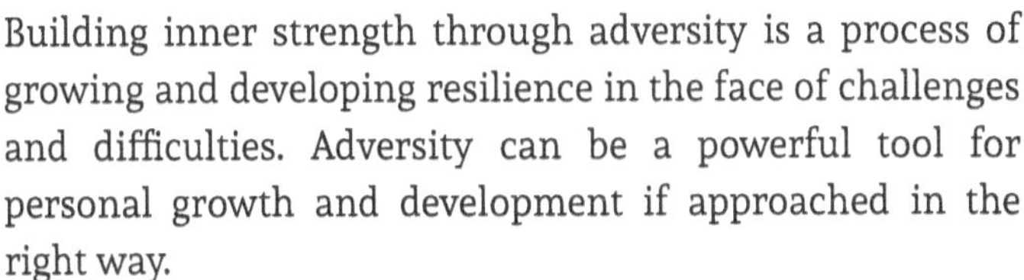

Building inner strength through adversity is a process of growing and developing resilience in the face of challenges and difficulties. Adversity can be a powerful tool for personal growth and development if approached in the right way.

One of the keys to building inner strength is to develop a growth mindset. This means embracing challenges and failures as opportunities for growth and learning. It also means seeing failures as temporary setbacks rather than permanent failures.

Another important aspect of building inner strength is developing a support system. This can include seeking out friends, family, or a therapist who can provide emotional support during difficult times.

It is also important to practice self-care and prioritize physical and mental health. This can involve engaging in activities such as exercise, mindfulness, or hobbies. Taking care of oneself can help to reduce stress and improve overall well-being.

Another way to build inner strength is to develop coping mechanisms for dealing with stress and challenges. This can include techniques such as deep breathing, progressive muscle relaxation, and visualization. Building a toolbox of coping strategies can help individuals to better manage stress and difficult emotions.

Finally, it is important to recognize and celebrate small victories and accomplishments. This can help to build confidence and resilience and provide a sense of accomplishment and satisfaction.

In conclusion, building inner strength through adversity requires a proactive approach that includes developing a growth mindset, seeking out a support system, practicing self-care, developing coping mechanisms, and celebrating small victories. With persistence and determination, individuals can develop the inner strength needed to overcome challenges and lead a fulfilling life.

𐡃𐡃𐡃

"I'm a great believer in luck, and I find the
harder I work, the more I have of it."

-Thomas Jefferson

♡♡♡

FOURTEEN

FINDING HOPE IN THE DARKEST OF TIMES

Finding hope in the darkest of times can be a difficult and challenging process, but it is essential for recovery and healing. Hope is a powerful motivator that can help individuals to persevere through difficult times and find meaning in life.

One of the first steps in finding hope is to identify what gives life meaning and purpose. This can involve exploring personal values, beliefs, and goals. By having a clear sense of purpose, individuals can find motivation and direction during difficult times.

It is also important to cultivate a positive mindset and focus on the present moment. This can involve practicing mindfulness and gratitude, and focusing on the good things in life. This can help to reduce stress and anxiety and provide a sense of peace and well-being.

Another way to find hope is to seek out a support system of friends, family, or a therapist. Having someone to talk to and confide in can provide a sense of comfort and emotional support during difficult times.

In addition, it is important to engage in self-care and prioritize physical and mental health. This can include engaging in exercise, eating a healthy diet, and getting adequate sleep. Taking care of oneself can help to reduce stress and improve overall well-being.

Lastly, it is important to find hope and meaning in small things. This can include finding joy in the simple things in life, such as spending time with loved ones, reading a good book, or listening to music.

In conclusion, finding hope in the darkest of times requires a proactive approach that involves identifying what gives life meaning and purpose, cultivating a positive mindset, seeking out a support system, engaging in self-care, and finding hope and meaning in small things. With persistence and determination, individuals can find hope and light in the darkest of times and lead a fulfilling life.

ᛈᛈᛈ

"The future belongs to those who believe in the beauty of their dreams."

-Eleanor Roosevelt

ᗗᗗᗗ

FIFTEEN

Conclusion Putting it All Together and Coping with Difficult Times

In conclusion, dealing with difficult times requires a comprehensive approach that includes understanding and managing trauma, building inner strength through adversity, and finding hope in the darkest of times. This involves seeking professional help, engaging in self-care, developing coping mechanisms, cultivating a positive mindset, and seeking out a support system.

It is important to remember that recovery and healing is a journey, not a destination, and that it may take time and effort. However, with persistence and determination, individuals can overcome adversity and lead a fulfilling life.

In difficult times, it is also important to be kind and compassionate towards oneself. It is okay to feel overwhelmed and to take things one day at a time. By taking small steps towards recovery and healing, individuals can build resilience and inner strength and find hope in the darkest of times.

In conclusion, coping with difficult times requires a proactive approach and a commitment to personal growth and development. With time and support, individuals can overcome adversity and lead a fulfilling life filled with hope and resilience.

ɒɒɒ

Other Books Of The Author

1. The Moments When I Met God
2. Kashiyile Theertha Pathangal
3. GURU GYAN VANI
4. Abhiprerak Gita
5. ASSI SE JAIN GHAT TAK
6. Hopelessness of Arjuna
7. The Soul and It's True Nature
8. Sense of Action (Karma)
9. Action through Wisdom
10. Action through Wisdom
11. THEORY AND PRACTICAL OF EVERY ACTION
12. LOGICAL UNDERSTANDING OF THE SUPREME
13. THE IMPERISHABLE SUPREME
14. Yatra Nishadraj se Hanuman Ghat Tak
15. Yatra Karnatak Ghat se Raja Ghat Tak
16. Yatra Pandey Ghat se Prayagraj Ghat Tak
17. Yatra Ranjendra Prasad Ghat se Dattatreya Ghat Tak
18. YaatraSindhiya Ghat se Gwaliar Ghat Tak
19. Yatra Mangala Gauri Ghat se Hanuman Gadhi Ghat Tak
20. Yatra Gaay Ghat Se Nishad Ghat Tak
21. MAA GANGA, GHATEN EVM UTSAV
22. Ganga Arti Dev Deepavali evam Any Utsav
23. Potentials of Digitalized India
24. VEDIC CONSCIOUSNESS
25. A Brief Introduction to Vedic Science
26. Kashi ke Barah Jyotirling
27. IMPACT OF MOTIVATION
28. Let's have a Milky Way Journey
29. Color Therapy in a Nutshell

ᐅᐅᐅ

Contact

DR. JAGADEESH PILLAI

MBA & PhD in Vedic Science

Four Times Guinness World Record Holder

Winner of Mahatma Gandhi Vishwa Shanti Puraskar and
Global Peace Ambassador

Gemology, Astro & Vastu Consultant - Spiritual Counselor

Consultant for designing World Record Ideas

Efficient Tarot Card Reader

9839093003

myrichindia@gmail.com

drjagadeeshpillai@facebook

drjagadeeshpillai@instagram
jagadeeshpillai@youtube

www. JAGADEESHPILLAI.com

ᗡᗡᗡ